The Human Body

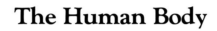

This edition first published in 1987 by Raintree Publishers Inc.

Text copyright © 1987 by Raintree Publishers Inc.
© 1982 Hachette

Library of Congress Number: 86-33869

1 2 3 4 5 6 7 8 9   94 93 92 91 90 89 88 87

Library of Congress Cataloging in Publication Data

Finifter, Germaine.
  Ask about the human body.

  Translation of: Mon corps.
  Summary: Answers questions about the human
body and how it works.
  1. Body, Human—Juvenile literature
[1. Body, Human. 2. Questions and answers]
I. Title. Human Anatomy
QP37.F5513 1987   612   86-33869
ISBN 0-8172-2884-5 (lib. bdg.)   C
ISBN 0-8172-2896-9 (softcover)

Cover illustration: David Schweitzer

Ask About
The Human Body

RAINTREE PUBLISHERS
Milwaukee

Contents

How the body works

A very special you

How the body works

How do people stand up?

A house has a framework which allows it to stand up. Each person has a framework of 206 bones in different shapes and sizes that make up a skeleton. Skeletons allow human beings to stand up. Some of these bones protect the delicate parts of the body like the lungs, heart, and brain.

What are bones made of?

Bones are hard and strong so that they won't break easily, but they are light enough to allow people to move around. The innermost part of most bones is made of bone marrow. The next layer is made of spongy bone which is covered with a layer of very hard ivory-like bone. Bones contain minerals. The most important mineral they contain is calcium.

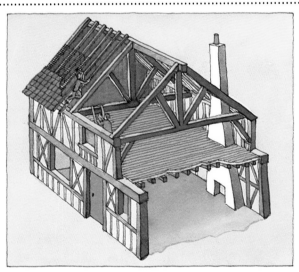

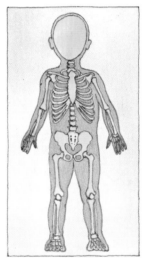

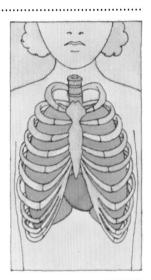

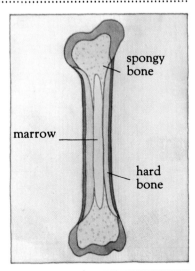

spongy
bone

marrow

hard
bone

Why can't babies stand up?

A newborn baby's bones are not strong enough for it to stand up, but the baby's tender bones will gradually change into hard bone. After several weeks, a baby will be able to hold its head up. At about seven months, he or she will be able to sit up. At one year, the baby will be able to stand.

How do bones grow?

There is growing tissue at each end of a child's bones. The tissue can stretch and grow longer. The part that stretches will eventually become hard and long. Children keep growing as long as their bones contain this growing tissue, usually until the end of their teen years.

What happens when people break an arm or leg?

If you fall, you may break an arm or a leg. An x-ray will show where the bone is broken. A doctor will put the broken bone back in place and apply a plaster cast to keep the bone still. After about three months, the bone will be healed.

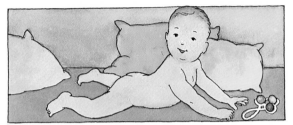

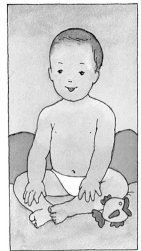

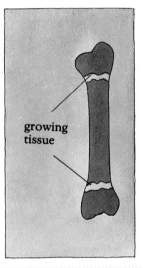

growing
tissue

6 yrs.

10 yrs.

18 yrs.

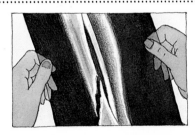

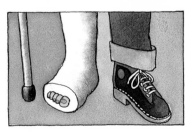

How do people move?

Bones join together to form joints. These joints allow you to bend your arms, legs, and fingers. You can lean, turn your head, or twist from the waist because of these joints. Smooth cartilage covers most of these joints to help them move smoothly.

How do arms and legs bend?

Your elbows and knees have hinge joints that work like the hinges of a door. Tough bands of tissue called ligaments fasten the bones together to help them bend.

How do arms move in circles?

A ball-and-socket joint connects the upper arm to the shoulder. It works on the same principle as a swivel lamp. The round end of the arm bone fits into a hollow in the shoulder. This allows the arm to swivel around. There is also a ball-and-socket joint in the hip.

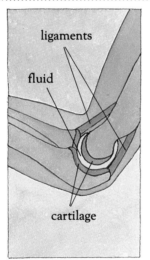

ligaments

fluid

cartilage

Why can't people turn their heads completely around?

Between the first two vertebrae at the base of the neck is a pivot joint which turns the head from side to side, but it is not possible to move the head completely around. The other vertebrae have joints which allow movement from front to back.

How do our mouths open and close?

People are able to move because of the muscles that are attached to their bones by tendons. When people decide to move their bodies (such as opening or closing their mouths), the brain tells the muscles what to do.

What do our hearts look like on the inside?

If a person's heart stops working, he or she will die. The heart is a muscle that works like a pump. Blood is pumped away from the heart by arteries, and the blood returns through veins.

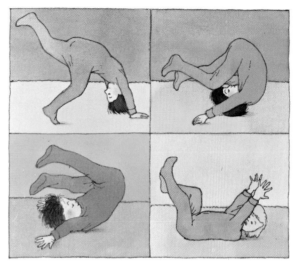

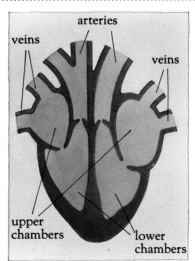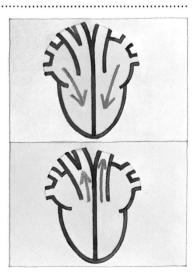

arteries

veins

veins

upper
chambers

lower
chambers

What makes our hearts beat?

Your heart beats about seventy times a minute when you are at rest. While you run or if you are frightened, it beats faster. The heart beats because parts of it contract and then relax. This makes blood flow in and out of the heart through valves that open and shut.

Why do we bleed when we hurt ourselves?

Blood flows around our bodies inside of large and small blood vessels. If a person falls, sometimes these blood vessels get torn and blood flows out. In time, the vessels will heal.

What is blood for?

An average adult has approximately six quarts of blood in his or her body. Blood has two jobs. It carries oxygen and dissolved food to all living cells in the body, and it carries waste material to the kidneys and lungs, which dispose of the waste.

Seventy heartbeats
a minute

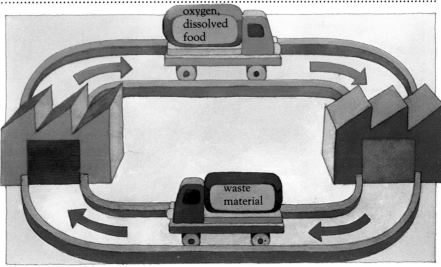

oxygen,
dissolved
food

waste
material

1
QUART

1
QUART

1
QUART

1
QUART

1
QUART

1
QUART

How does blood circulate?

In a home, clean water enters through a series of pipes. The water is used and becomes dirty. The dirty water leaves through another set of pipes. The human body has a similar system. Oxygen-carrying blood leaves the heart through the arteries and the blood returns through the veins.

Why is blood red?

Blood contains red and white blood cells. Red blood cells have a substance called hemoglobin which gives blood its red color and carries oxygen to cells. If blood is bright red, it has a good supply of oxygen. If blood is dark red, there is not enough oxygen and the person feels tired.

What are lungs for?

Lungs are on either side of the heart. When you breathe in, your lungs fill with air. When you breathe out, your lungs empty. Air is made up of many gases including oxygen and carbon dioxide. Blood absorbs oxygen and gets rid of the carbon dioxide which your body cannot use.

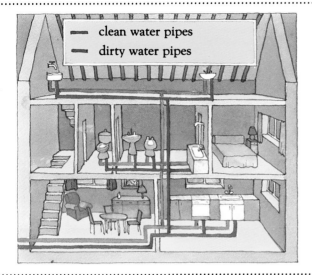

clean water pipes
dirty water pipes

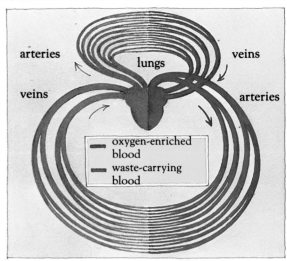

arteries   lungs   veins

veins   arteries

oxygen-enriched blood
waste-carrying blood

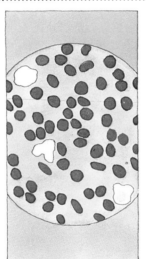

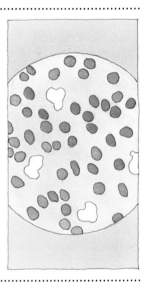

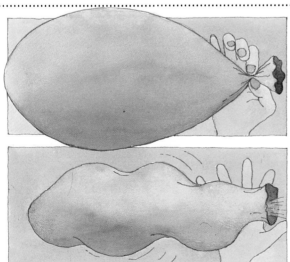

How does air get inside of our lungs?

Your chest contains muscles between the ribs and a larger muscle known as the diaphragm. When the muscles contract, a big space is left and air is breathed in automatically. The air enters through your mouth and nose and goes down your throat and windpipe. The windpipe divides in two, and each of these pipes joins one of the lungs.

Why do we have hair inside our noses?

Inside of each person's nose there are hundreds of tiny hairs. These hairs act as filters to keep harmful bits of dust and germs from entering the lungs. For this reason, you should always try to breathe through your nose rather than your mouth. Sneezing helps to clear your nose, too.

Why do people have to eat?

Just as gasoline makes a car's engine run, food provides energy for muscles, lungs, and other parts of the human body.

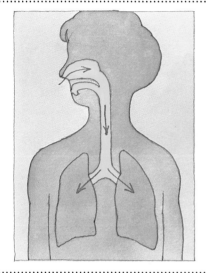

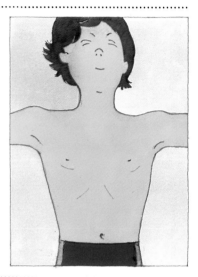

What would happen if you only ate food from cans?

You should eat fresh fruit and vegetables every day. They contain vitamins and minerals needed for good health. Long ago, people who ate no fresh food were lacking in vitamin C and got a serious illness called scurvy.

Why do people get white patches on their nails?

If people have white patches on their nails or if their nails break easily, it is a sign that they need more calcium. Calcium is a mineral necessary for strong bones, teeth, and nails. Milk and milk products such as cheese and butter contain calcium. They also contain vitamin D which is necessary for growth.

Why do people have teeth?

Newborn babies do not have teeth. They are fed only liquids. They can start to eat solid food (chopped or strained) once they get their baby teeth. After a while, these baby teeth are pushed out by adult teeth that replace them. An adult has thirty-two teeth—eight incisors for biting food, four canines for tearing food, and eight premolars and twelve molars for chewing food.

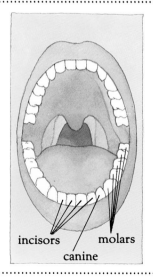

incisors   molars
    canine

23

Why don't the adult teeth get pushed out, too?

If you take care of your teeth, they will be strong and should last all your life. The visible part of each tooth is called the crown, and it is made of bonelike material with an outer layer of enamel. You can't see the root which attaches the tooth to your jaw. Each tooth is a living part of your body, and each contains blood vessels and nerves.

What is saliva?

Saliva is a liquid made by glands inside of the mouth. It is important to the digestive process. Saliva lubricates food that you have chewed so that the food is easier to swallow.

Why do people have tongues?

Your teeth chew food, and then saliva turns it into a soft paste. Your tongue shapes the food into a ball and sends it down your throat. Your tongue also tells you how things taste and is important for speaking.

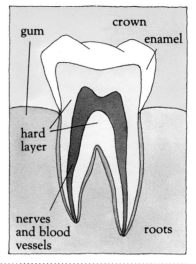

gum

crown

enamel

hard layer

nerves and blood vessels

roots

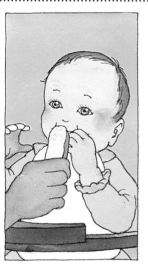

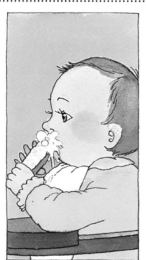

How does the stomach work?

Your stomach works like a food processor. Food in the stomach is churned up by muscles and mixed with special juices. When the food becomes liquid, it is sent on to the small intestine.

What is indigestion?

Sometimes you might eat the wrong thing or too much of something, and your stomach becomes upset. You feel better when the food passes through your system and eventually leaves your body. In the small intestine, blood absorbs most of the food and water needed by the body. The rest of the food that the body does not need moves into the large intestine. This waste is collected in the rectum, and your body gets rid of it when you go to the bathroom.

What is the pupil of the eye?

The front of the eye is protected by a clear skin called the cornea. In the center of the cornea is a colored circle known as the iris. At the center of the iris is a black opening called the pupil. In order for you to see, rays of light must pass through the pupil to the retina at the back of the eye.

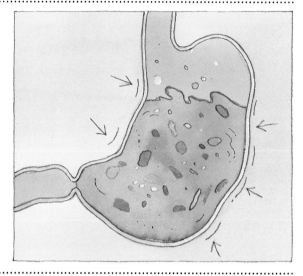

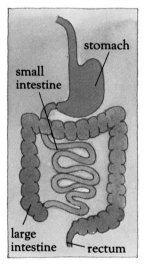

stomach

small intestine

large intestine

rectum

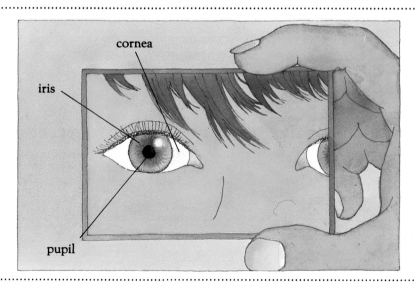

cornea

iris

pupil

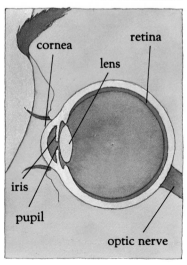

cornea

retina

lens

iris

pupil

optic nerve

102729

How do people see?

Your eyes need light of some kind in order for you to see. The rays of light pass through the pupil and touch the retina which makes the nerves send messages to the brain.

Why must some people wear glasses?

People who have difficulty seeing things far away are nearsighted. People who have difficulty seeing things close are farsighted. If you have any difficulty seeing, you need to visit an eye doctor called an ophthalmologist. The doctor will prescribe glasses (or contact lenses) to correct your vision.

Why do some children squint?

There are six muscles in each eye that allow the eye to look up and down and side to side. If one of the muscles is too strong or too weak, the eyes do not work together which causes a squint. A squint can be corrected with glasses, exercises, or perhaps minor surgery.

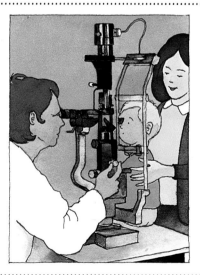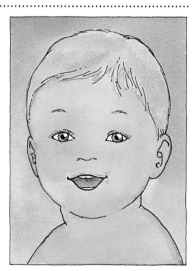

How do people go blind?

Some people are born blind. An accident or an illness, however, can cause a person to go blind later in life. A person is blind if the images received by the retina can no longer be sent to the brain. You should always be very careful to protect your eyes during all of your daily activities.

How do we close our eyes?

Closing your eyes is like closing the curtains to darken a room. Your eyes close when your brain tells your muscles to lower your eyelids. If your eyes get into danger, you close them quickly or blink to protect them.

How do people speak?

You have vocal cords inside your throat in the part called the voice box or larynx. These vocal cords vibrate when air passes over them in the same way that a harmonica works. When you want to speak or sing, you breathe in over your vocal cords, and the vibration causes sound. You shape the sound with your lips, mouth, teeth, and tongue.

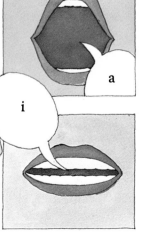
a

e

u

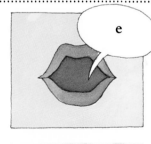
i

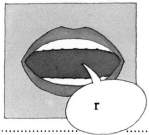
r

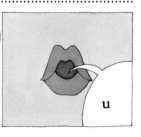
t

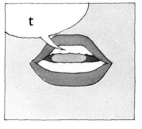

How do we hear?

The outside of your ear leads inside to an eardrum which is made of thin skin. When sounds picked up by your ear touch the eardrum, it vibrates. These vibrations travel further down the ear to three big bones. A nerve there sends the vibrations to the brain which tells you what was heard.

Why are some people deaf?

If you make a noise behind a baby, he or she will react by turning around. You know that the baby can hear. Sometimes, however, a baby is deaf. The baby may have been born deaf. Accidents and illness can also cause deafness or hearing loss. It is important that you get your hearing tested to see if it is normal.

How do nerves work?

Nerves branch out to all parts of the body from the base of the brain. They reach every bit of muscle, skin, and bone. These nerves send signals that they receive to the brain, and then return instructions from the brain. If you touch something hot, for instance, your nerves tell the muscles in your hand to pull away quickly.

auditory
nerve

eardrum

outer
ear

What does the brain look like?

The brain has two parts that join together. The brain is made of gray tissue that bends and folds. It contains millions of nerve cells. Each cell is part of a chain. Chains of cells are grouped together to form cables called nerves. Certain parts of the brain are devoted to different things including movement, smell, speech, hearing, sight, and feeling.

How does the brain work?

Imagine that everyone's telephone is connected to a main telephone station. The main station constantly receives calls through cables from the houses and connects them to other houses. The brain works in the same way. It sends and receives messages to and from different parts of the body through nerves.

What other things does the brain do?

The brain is the main station for movement, thought, memory, and feelings. One part of the brain is in charge of your balance and coordination. Another part is in charge of breathing, digestion, and heartbeat. Another part deals with your thoughts and activities. Other parts allow you to see, hear, feel, smell, and taste.

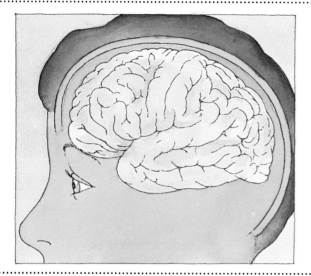

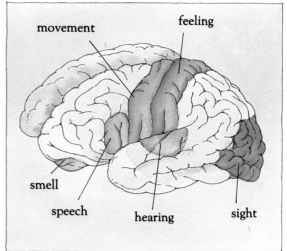

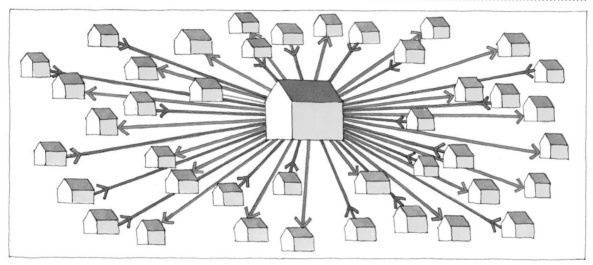

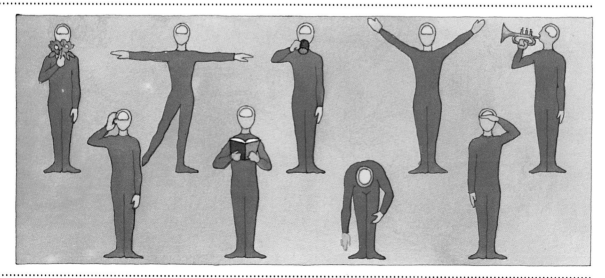

Why are some people right-handed and some left-handed?

In most people, the left side of the brain is more developed than the right. The left side of the brain controls the right side of the body. That is why most people are right-handed. Sometimes, though, the right side of the brain is more developed, and that person is left-handed. Either way is perfectly fine.

How does hair grow?

Your hair has roots underneath your scalp. Hair grows because the roots are fed by blood vessels. Hair grows almost a half an inch every month.

Do nails grow even if you break them?

Your nails will continue to grow after you trim them or if you should break one. Your nails are very important because they protect the ends of your fingers, thumbs, and toes.

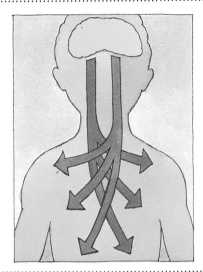

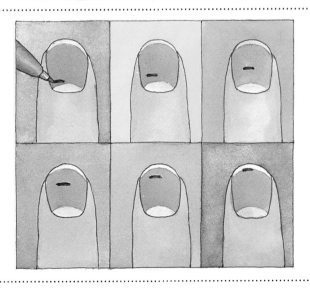

A very special you

Why can only men grow beards?

Men are able to grow beards because their bodies produce certain hormones that allow hair to grow on the face and chest. Women do not produce these hormones, and so their skin is smooth. Men can shave their facial hair completely or shape some of it into a beard or mustache.

Why are males different from females?

All living things (plants, animals, and people) were first formed when a male and a female cell joined together. There are two different sexes (male and female) because each has a job to do in order for a new plant, animal, or person to be created.

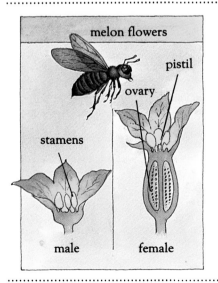

melon flowers

pistil

ovary

stamens

male

female

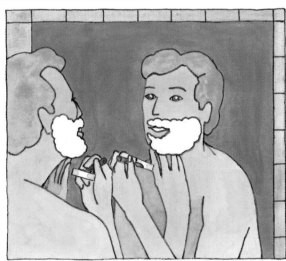

Why don't men have babies?

A man's body is not made to grow a baby. A woman has a special place in her body called a womb for growing babies.

How is a baby formed?

A man's body produces a liquid that contains sperm. A woman's body has two ovaries which produce female cells called eggs. When a sperm joins with an egg, it can grow into a baby inside the mother's body. The egg is "fertilized," and the mother is "pregnant."

What if a woman does not want to become pregnant?

Women who do not want to become pregnant use birth control. There are many forms of birth control available from a doctor. A common method is in the form of a pill. Birth control prevents the father's sperm from fertilizing the mother's egg.

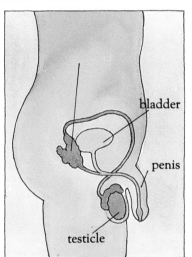

bladder

penis

testicle

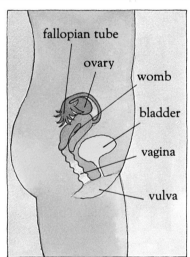

fallopian tube

ovary

womb

bladder

vagina

vulva

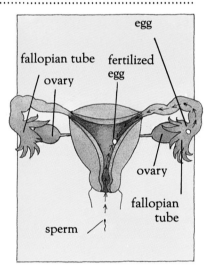

fallopian tube

ovary

fertilized egg

egg

ovary

fallopian tube

sperm

How does the fertilized egg turn into a baby?

The fertilized egg forms a ball of cells and attaches itself to the wall of the mother's womb. The ball is fed by the mother's body, and it grows into a baby.

How long does it take to grow into a baby?

It takes nine months for the fertilized egg to grow into a baby. The head, heart, legs, and arms are formed in the first two months. In the beginning of the third month, it has a mouth, eyes, and ears. It will grow bigger each day for the remaining months.

Why do some mothers give birth to twins?

Sometimes the fertilized egg divides in two, and both eggs develop in the same sac. This produces identical twins. If two sperm meet two eggs, the babies develop in separate sacs. These babies will not be identical.

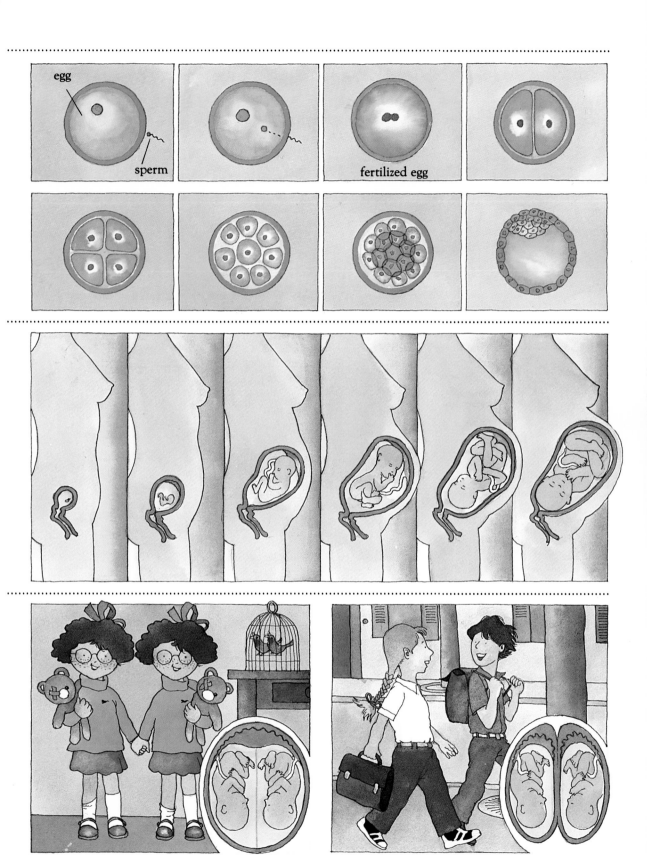

egg

sperm

fertilized egg

How does the mother know when it is time for her baby to be born?

When you make a fist, you contract your muscles. When a baby is ready to be born, muscles in the womb contract in the same way. The mother should then go to the hospital. As it gets nearer to the time for the baby to be born, the contractions become stronger and more frequent.

What does the baby eat?

Newborn babies drink milk from the mother's body. Eventually the baby is fed milk from a bottle. As the baby grows, it will begin to eat strained, chopped, and solid food.

What makes up the human body?

Just as millions and trillions of grains of sand make up a beach, the human body is made of trillions of cells. There are approximately seventy-five trillion tiny nerve cells, bone cells, muscle cells, sex cells, skin cells, brain cells, and so on in the human body. They are visible only under a microscope.

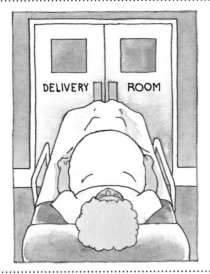

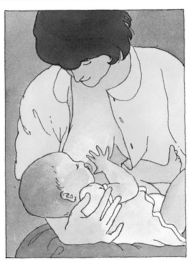

There are
millions of
grains of sand
in a
sandcastle.

There are
seventy-five
trillion cells in
the human body.

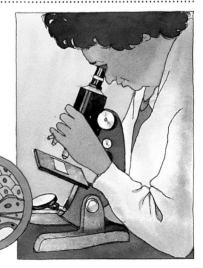

**Why are babies
sometimes girls
and sometimes boys?**

Parents can't choose whether to have a boy or a girl. It is determined by chromosomes. Tiny threads called chromosomes make up the center of cells in your body. In a female sex cell, all the chromosomes look alike and are in the shape of an **X.** In the male sex cell, all the chromosomes are in the shape of an **X** except one; it is in the shape of a **Y.** If two **X** chromosomes join together, the baby will be a girl. If an **X** and a **Y** join, the baby will be a boy.

**Why do people
look different
from each other?**

Each chromosome is made of tiny particles called genes. Genes determine a person's shape and personality. Each person inherits genes from both parents. Nobody else has those exact same genes so no two people are identical in every way. Children in the same family may look similar, however. Identical twins share the same genes so they look alike.

**Why do people
have different
skin colors?**

A long time ago, people who lived in hot climates developed darker skin to protect them from the sun. Today, people of different colors live all over the world. The color of your skin is determined by your genes.

female sex cell   male sex cell

It's a girl!

female sex cell   male sex cell

It's a boy!

Smith Family

Son

Smith Fam...

Fathe...

Smith Fam...

Grandma

Smith Family

Grandpa

Brown Family

Smith Family

Father

...ily

...Family

Mother

Jones Family

Jones Family

Jones Family

Daughter

**Why do some
people have
freckles?**

Again, your genes decide whether or not you have freckles. People with freckles usually also have fair skin and red or blond hair. Freckles darken with exposure to the sun. They fade in winter but never completely disappear.

**Why do some
people have
beauty marks?**

Beauty marks are inherited from parents and can be found on various parts of the body. They are usually present at birth. Some people think that beauty marks are so attractive that they paint them on with makeup.

**Why are children
of the same age
sometimes
different heights?**

Children may be the same age, but height is determined by several factors. Height is affected by the kind of food you eat and your habits as you are growing up, and whether your family tends to be short, medium, or tall.

Why are some people extremely tall and some people extremely small?

There is a gland at the base of everyone's skull that produces a hormone for growth. In some people, that gland may not work properly. It may produce too much of the hormone, making the person very tall, or not enough of the hormone, making the person very small.

Why do people become tired?

In order to replace the energy that you've used during the day, you need a good night's sleep every night. You also need to eat good food. If you don't, you will feel tired. Sometimes when you are full of energy, you play extra hard. Your muscles, nerves, and heart work very hard, and afterwards you will need to rest.

Why do people get ill?

Sometimes people feel ill when one of their organs—the stomach, lungs, intestines, and so on—is not working properly. At other times, germs may have entered their bodies. The human body usually knows how to fight germs. Doctors prescribe medicines to get rid of germs, too.

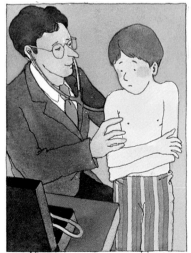

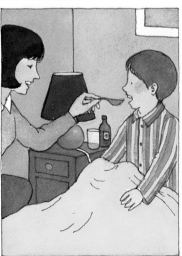

51

Why do people get stomachaches?

Sometimes food may be badly prepared or full of germs, and it gives you a stomachache. Or you may eat too much or too quickly and get a stomachache. Your stomach aches because your digestive system has to work harder to break down the food. When digestion is too slow or too fast, it causes pain.

What is appendicitis?

The appendix is a very small part of your body located in the lower right side of your abdomen. If it becomes infected or irritated, it can cause an illness known as appendicitis. The infected appendix may have to be removed through surgery.

What are warts?

Warts are small growths usually found on the fingers or soles of the feet. Warts can often be removed with medicine, but sometimes a doctor may have to remove them. Occasionally, they disappear all by themselves.

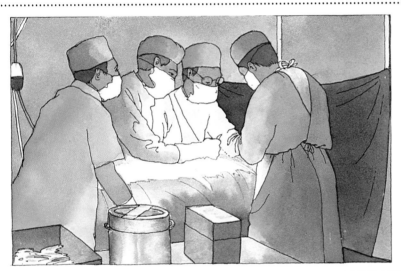

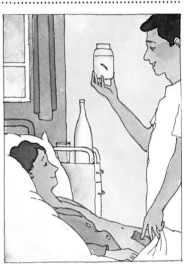

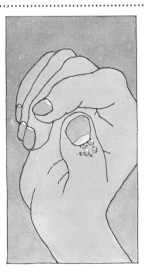

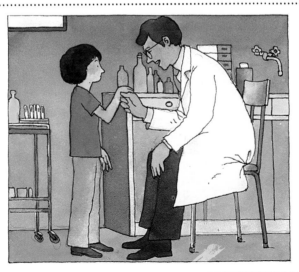

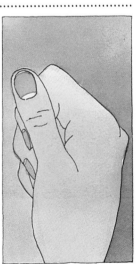

What are tonsils for?

Tonsils, located at the back of the throat, produce white blood cells that destroy germs. Sometimes tonsils become painful, and they may have to be removed. Once tonsils have been removed, the body will use other ways to fight germs.

Why do doctors use instruments to examine patients?

Instruments that doctors use are special tools that gather information about your body. Instruments are also used to perform operations and to repair broken bones. A doctor can listen inside your chest with a stethoscope. The doctor can see how your heart is working with an electrocardiograph. X-rays allow the doctor to see the organs and bones inside your body.

How does medicine help to make you well?

Medicine fights germs and relieves pain. A doctor will prescribe the medicine you need to make you feel better. Never take medicine on your own. A trusted adult will give you the medicine that you may need. Some medicines need to be swallowed. Other medicines are injected or applied to the skin.

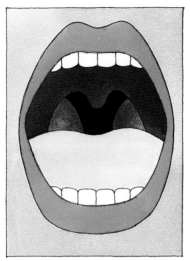

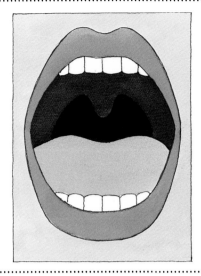

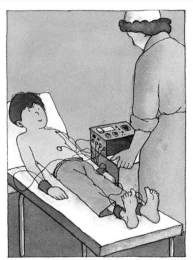

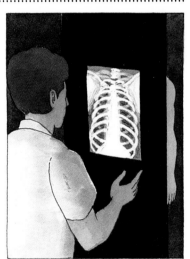

DANGER!
<u>Never</u> help yourself
to
pills or medicine!

Why are some people nice and some people mean?

A child who is healthy and who grows up with love and his or her needs fulfilled, will usually be a nice person. A person who acts mean may have had a difficult life or may be ill. Maybe the person really doesn't know why he or she is unhappy and can't explain it to others. This may make the person feel irritable and be unpleasant.

Is smoking bad for you?

Yes, smoking is very bad for your heart and lungs. Because it is hard to give up smoking, the wise person will never start.

What happens to people's bodies when they become frightened?

If something very frightening happens or you are startled, your heart beats faster and stronger. Your body produces a large quantity of a substance called adrenalin. Adrenalin prepares the body "to fight or to take flight."

Why do people age?

All through your life, the trillions of cells in your body are constantly being replaced by new ones. If you should cut yourself, this is how the cut is able to heal. People begin to age when their cells are not replaced with quite so many new cells.

Why does an adult's hair turn white or gray?

Hair color is determined by the coloring of the hair's roots. As people age, the coloring might stop being produced because the cells are not replaced.

Why do older people's fingers get stiff?

As people grow older, the number of bone cells that they have decreases. When this happens, the bones weaken and break more easily. The joints may ache or become less flexible. Your whole skeleton will change as you get older. You may even become a bit shorter.

Why do some people live longer than others?

If someone in your family has lived to be a hundred, it is likely that others in your family will live a long life, too. The length of your life will also depend on how well you take care of yourself. If you eat good food, get plenty of exercise, practice cleanliness, and get enough sleep, chances are you will live a good, long life.

Why do living things die?

A beautiful flower begins as a seed which sprouts and grows. The flower gradually blooms but later fades and dies. It is hard to understand, but this is the way of all living things—plants, animals, and humans. Fortunately, human beings have memories. Even though people you love might die, your memories will allow them to live on in your heart.

What is the point of living?

You have been given a gift—a gift of life—and it is your responsibility to make the most of it. It is your job to give life its meaning. If you look, life has much to give you; and you have much to offer. It is a good feeling to seek and find happiness. It also feels good to share in other people's happiness as well as to enjoy your own.

Glossary

bone marrow—the innermost part of most bones (p. 8)

chromosomes—tiny threads that make up the center of cells in the body (p. 46)

cornea—a clear skin that protects the front of the eye (p. 26)

crown—the visible part of a tooth made of bonelike material with an outer layer of enamel (p. 24)

hemoglobin—a substance found in blood that gives blood its red color and carries oxygen to cells (p. 18)

hormones—a product manufactured by the body that has a stimulatory effect on the activity of cells (p. 38)

joints—the point in arms, legs, and fingers where the different bones join together (p. 12)

ophthalmologist—a medical doctor who specializes in the structure, functions, and diseases of the eye (p. 28)

saliva—a liquid made by glands inside the mouth that helps in the digestive process (p. 24)

scurvy—a disease caused by a lack of vitamin C (p. 22)

vertebrae—bony segments that make up the spinal column (p. 14)

x-ray—a photographic process that allows bones and organs to be viewed and studied (p. 10)

Index